A PHOTOGRAPHIC HISTORY of
MINING IN SOUTH WALES

Two South Wales collieries became one on 8 November 1974, when Abercynon and Lady Windsor were linked underground. Haydn Gibbon, manager of Abercynon, is seen here shaking hands with Sam Rawlings, manager of Lady Windsor. Looking on is Gerard Timpt, site manager for the contractors Thyssen (GB) Ltd. (*Western Mail and Echo*)

A PHOTOGRAPHIC HISTORY of
MINING IN SOUTH WALES

JOHN O'SULLIVAN

First published in the United Kingdom in 2001 by Sutton Publishing Limited
This new paperback edition first published in 2011 by The History Press

Reprinted 2012

The History Press
The Mill, Brimscombe Port,
Stroud, Gloucestershire, GL5 2QG
www.thehistorypress.co.uk

British Library Cataloguing in Publication Data
A catalogue record for this book is available from the British Library.

ISBN 978-0-7524-5941-7

Illustrations

Front endpaper: In 1958 a major development took place at Hafodyrnys Colliery. It included new railway sidings, workshops, preparation plants and the enlarging of pithead baths. (*Western Mail and Echo*)
Back endpaper: Nantgarw Colliery, one of the South Wales show pits, 1962. (*Western Mail and Echo*)
Half-title page: Twelve-year-old John Davies after his first day of work as an underground door boy at Ferndale Colliery, 1910. (*Western Mail and Echo* Archives)
Title page: The winding gear at Penallta Colliery, near Ystrad Mynach. (*Western Mail and Echo*)

Dedication
*This book is dedicated to the generations
of miners and their families in South Wales
and to the victims, and families, of the
Aberfan disaster.*

Typeset in 11/14pt Photina.
Printed and bound in Great Britain by
Marston Book Services Limited, Didcot

One of the souvenir miners' lamps presented to members of the Wales rugby team which won the Triple Crown in 1905. (*Western Mail and Echo Archives*)

Contents

Men at Yniscedwyn drift mine, near Ystradgynlais, who made headlines when they refused to transfer to Abernant Colliery because it would have meant them going 2,000ft underground. (*Western Mail and Echo Archives*)

Introduction

When I mentioned to a friend, former librarian Barry Tobin, that I was compiling a history of the South Wales coal industry, he commented: 'So you will still be writing about religious affairs' – something which I have done for more than forty years. Barry continued: 'The Benedictine monks at Margam Abbey were the first miners in South Wales.'

With the help of Neath Port Talbot Library and Information Services I was able to confirm what Barry had told me. The library provided me with extracts from a book, *Pioneers of the Welsh Coalfield*, published by the *Western Mail* in 1925. In it the author, Elizabeth Phillips, referred to evidence that coal was worked in Felin Fach, Llanfabon, in 1283. She also stated that monks were probably the first diggers of coal in South Wales, 'for it is on record that the monks at Neath Abbey were getting coal for iron-making in the 13th Century', she wrote.

In *Birch's History of Margam Abbey*, it is recorded that a deed signed by Owen ap Alayth in 1284 granted a number of privileges to Margam Abbey. The donor gave all the stony coal under his land and the land of his men, together with the right of ingress and egress for two- and four-wheeled carts and other conveyances for a mark beforehand and half a crannock of wheat a year, as long as the monks used the coal; in return they undertook to compensate him for all damage done to his arable land by their digging for coal.

Elizabeth Phillips also referred to a collection of early charters published by Colonel Grant-Francis, including one given by William de Breos, the Norman lord, in 1305. This empowered the tenant to dig pit coal at Byllwasted, in the Swansea area, without hindrance by de Breos. In those early days the Crown exercised a prerogative over all mines and miners, and Edward I directed that a tithe of all the ore dug out of the Welsh mines should be paid to the parish churches of the neighbourhood.

According to Elizabeth Phillips, there is no written evidence that the Romans made use of coal when they occupied Britain, but excavations at a Roman villa discovered near Caerleon in 1883 produced evidence showing that coal had been used under the tessellated pavement.

It was not until the nineteenth century that coal became the main industry in South Wales, with coal owners making vast fortunes by exploiting miners. Men, women and children were little more than slaves, working long hours for little or no pay, their pitiful reward being in the form of tokens which could only be spent in the truck shops operated by their employers.

Reports in the Newport-based newspaper *The Merlin* in 1830 highlighted the problems of truck shops operated by coal owners and steel magnates in South Wales. Although the government had passed legislation outlawing truck shops, the bosses in South Wales still carried out the practice.

The late Ness Edwards, who later became MP for Caerphilly, referred to the issue in his book *South Wales Miners*, which was published in 1926. He described a petition that was sent to the Home Office on 3 April 1830, asking for the practice to be

Surface workers at the Albion Colliery on 23 June 1894, the day that 290 men and boys were killed in an explosion. (*Western Mail and Echo Archives*)

stamped out. Seven days later the matter came to a head. *The Merlin* reported that a large number of workers had gathered at Pentwyn Mawr – between Crumlin and Blackwood – to discuss the price of food. The local mine owner, Mr Fothergill, then rode up on his horse and demanded to know why they were not at work. One of the miners told him they were not satisfied with the truck system of paying in goods instead of money, particularly with regard to food. The spokesman claimed they were forced to pay 20 to 30 per cent more in the company shops than in other shops in the adjoining market towns. The men proposed that they should be paid in money, ten shillings a week and the balance fortnightly.

The following week the employers agreed to a number of concessions: to keep coal up to a fair market price; to reduce the quantity brought down; and to pay the men as proposed at the Pentwyn Mawr meeting. The truck system was abolished in the area, but still operated in other parts of South Wales.

When the miners returned to work, the men at Crumlin were told that their wages were to be reduced. The men were ready. They had already decided that no one was to work at reduced rates.

Early in May a mass meeting was held at Crosspenmaen. The delegates agreed that men who refused to work at reduced rates and failed to get alternative employment would be supported by miners who were working. A treasurer was appointed, together with a collector for each pit, forming the first miners' lodges.

The loose organisations of those early days were the forerunners of the miners' unions which emerged over decades. Mr Crawshaw and Mr Fothergill were already having second thoughts about scrapping the scheme as without the truck shops their profits fell.

Shopkeepers in areas where the truck shops were still open then petitioned Parliament. They claimed that the paying of wages in truck was not only a violation of

William Thomas Williams, Harold Smallcombe and David Jones, pictured in the backyard of a house in King Street, Gelli, Rhondda, after their first day's work underground. The oldest, William, was only thirteen. (*Western Mail and Echo Archives*)

the law but a gross and cruel infringement on every class that contributed directly or indirectly to the support of the State. The petition went on: 'The truck system deprives tradesmen of legitimate custom, depreciates the value of property, disables the money-making manufacturers from fair competition, enslaves the workman and exposes him without any remedy to all the fraud and oppression which has invariably accompanied the truck system.'

As the anger grew over the truck system and the government's controversial Reform Bill, soldiers were sent to Merthyr early in June 1831 to disperse a mass meeting of miners which had been called to decide on strike action. While Mr Guest, the ironmaster, in his role as sheriff, was reading the Riot Act, the workers attacked and disarmed the soldiers. For the next five days, South Wales was in the hands of the miners. Soldiers were drafted into the area from many parts of the country and gradually regained control. Many miners were thrown into prison and their leader, Dick Penderyn, was hanged at Cardiff on 13 August 1831, allegedly for the fatal stabbing of Duncan Black. A plaque outside Cardiff market marks the place where Penderyn died. On the 170th anniversary of Penderyn's death, 13 August 2001, a memorial ceremony was held near the plaque and the tributes were led by First Minister Rhoderi Morgan. He echoed the view held by generations of

The South Wales Miners' Federation window at the former offices in St Andrew's Crescent, Cardiff. (*Western Mail and Echo Archives*)

Miners' leader, William Abraham MP, known as Mabon. (*Treorchy Library*)

people in South Wales: that Penderyn was innocent and was a true martyr of the fight for workers' rights.

Another giant in the struggle for miners' rights was William Abraham, known as Mabon (probably his Bardic name), the first president of the South Wales Miners' Federation. He was born at Cwmafan on 14 June 1842, and died at Pentre, Rhondda, on 14 May 1922. After leaving Cwmafan National School he became a tin-plater but switched to mining, where he worked as a door boy.

In 1870 he was elected as a miners' agent and played a prominent part in the struggle which led in 1875 to the drawing-up of a sliding scale of wages in the coalfields, linked to prices and profits. From 1892 to 1898 miners did not work on the first Monday of each month, as part of a scheme to limit output and maintain wages. This day was known as Mabon's Monday, and gave the miners the opportunity to hold meetings to discuss their grievances.

In 1885 Mabon was elected MP for the Rhondda Division, becoming the first miners' representative from South Wales to sit in the House of Commons. He was a member of the radical wing of the Liberal Party until 1906 when the Labour Party became a

The Salvation Army conducted a funeral for one of their members after the Senghenydd Pit disaster in 1913.

separate political party. The Miners' Federation affiliated to the Labour Party in 1909. Mabon did not take a very active part in political life, although he represented Rhondda West for the Labour Party from 1918 until his death, shortly before his 80th birthday, in 1922. He played a much greater role in the history of the trade union movement in Wales. As Ness Edwards recorded: 'In the early days the miners were loosely organised in a number of small and independent local bodies. Mabon strove to preserve their autonomy, despite the campaign by younger miners to form a more unified and firmly knit organisation. The young brigade won the day when the South Wales Miners' Federation was formed in 1898. Mabon was elected its first president. In this role he preached moderation and was a conciliating influence on his followers, but he failed to prevent the series of critical disputes which led to the first general miners' strike in 1912.

Outside the mining industry and politics, Mabon was also a great supporter of the Eisteddfod and his burly appearance and booming voice were features of events at the end of the nineteenth century and the beginning of the twentieth. He conducted choirs and, as a noted tenor, often sang to the vast crowds attending the festivals. Mabon, who was made a Privy Councillor in 1911, was married for forty years to Sarah Williams, who died in 1900. They had three sons and three daughters.

The constant friction between miners and managers continued over the generations, with the General Strike in 1926 and the hunger marches of the 1930s. The nationalisation of the coal industry on 1 January 1947 failed to bridge completely the gap between management and men. There was the fight against closures in the 1950s, the dispute which brought down Prime Minister Ted Heath's Conservative government in the 1970s and the year-long strike in the 1980s when the National Union of Miners failed to stop Margaret Thatcher's government, and its henchman Ian McGregor, from all but destroying the coal industry, especially in South Wales. At the end of the twentieth century there was only one surviving deep pit, Tower Colliery, Hirwain. This was saved in 1994 by a workers buy-out led by Tyrone O'Sullivan and fellow members of the NUM.

History shows that the men of Tower – and their families – were following a tradition of determination which started in 1831, when the Swansea Yeomanry were ambushed and disarmed. In his booklet *The Tower Story*, Professor Hywel Francis, whose father was Dai Francis, long-serving secretary of the South Wales NUM, said that in 1831 the miners and ironworkers at Hirwaun sacrificed a calf, washed a flag in its blood and used it as a war banner. It was the first known occasion when the Red Flag was used as a symbol of revolt in Britain. On 12 April 1962 nine men were killed in an explosion at Tower. In 1963 David John O'Sullivan, Tyrone's father, died in a roof fall at the colliery.

While the coal owners made fortunes over the generations, hundreds of miners paid for the black diamonds with their lives. The worst disaster was at Universal Pit, Senghenydd, in 1913, when 439 men died in an underground explosion. The saddest incident was on 21 October 1966, when a landslide of waste from Merthyr Vale Colliery destroyed a school and houses and left 144 people, including 116 children, dead in the village of Aberfan. I covered the disaster for the *Daily Mail* and the horror of what happened still haunts me thirty-five years later. I was at the inquest when John Collins, whose wife and two sons had died in the incident, screamed at the coroner Ben Hamilton: 'The only verdict is murdered by the National Coal Board.' John later told me that his father, himself a miner, had wept with joy when the industry was nationalised. 'Now I weep with sorrow and anger at what happened at Aberfan,' he said.

Between them, the miners and the coal owners made Cardiff the greatest coal-exporting port in the world, its foundations built around a community that was a village at the beginning of the nineteenth century, a prosperous town at the turn of that century, a city in 1905 and the capital city of Wales in 1955. Yet it was only in the mid-1990s, when there was just one deep pit operating in South Wales, that the miners were given the Freedom of the City of Cardiff. It was an honour that was long overdue.

My home town of Barry was also a coal-rush town at the end of the nineteenth century and the beginning of the twentieth. My great-grandfather was the skipper of one of the hundreds of ships which carried coal from Barry. My grandfather, Patrick O'Sullivan, jumped his ship to become a coal trimmer at Barry.

There may be only one deep pit operating in South Wales at the start of the twenty-first century but miners are still front-page news. Hundreds of men are now fighting for compensation for the coal dust in their lungs, a relic of the years they spent working underground. Widows of men who died from the killer dust were also seeking payments. The government is said to be paying out up to a million pounds a day.

The Early Days

The miners of Merthyr and Rhymney helped to elect Keir Hardy as
the first Labour MP, but it was the Durham miners who adopted
Hardy as the hero for their area banner.
(*Western Mail and Echo Archives*)

These women worked at Bwllfa Colliery, Aberdare, around 1870. (*Western Mail and Echo Archives*)

Men, women and children queuing at a pawn shop in South Wales during a miners' strike in the mid-1870s. (*Western Mail and Echo Archives*)

Women working at Abergorki Colliery, Treorchy, in 1850. (*Western Mail and Echo Archives*)

Dinas Middle Colliery, shortly after it started production in 1879. (*Western Mail and Echo Archives*)

South Griffin Colliery, Blaina, which was opened in 1883 and closed in 1920. (*Western Mail and Echo Archives*)

Miners and hauliers with their ponies at the Ton Pentre level around 1890. (*Western Mail and Echo Archives*)

Men who worked the first shift at the Arrael Griffin Colliery pit which was sunk at Six Bells, Abertillery, in 1896. (*Western Mail and Echo Archives*)

Men at Deep Navigation Colliery, Treharris, in the early twentieth century. (*Western Mail and Echo Archives*)

A group at Penrhiw Colliery in 1904, during the period when the 'religious revival' swept through the South Wales Coalfield. (*Western Mail and Echo Archives*)

Strikers waiting to enter the Empire Theatre, Tonypandy, on 9 November 1910. (*Western Mail and Echo Archives*)

Cambrian Colliery strikers, 1910/11. (*Western Mail and Echo Archives*)

Policemen guarding the Pontypridd magistrates' court where strikers were appearing, believed to be on Boxing Day, 1910. (*Western Mail and Echo Archives*)

Pit sinkers at the Ynyscorrwg Colliery, Glyncorrwg, 1912. They were dressed in waterproof clothing and wore leather helmets, which had a big flap covering part of their shoulders and neck. (*Western Mail and Echo Archives*)

Men and boys signing on at Nantgarw Colliery in this undated photograph. (*Western Mail and Echo Archives*)

A screen and cleaning belts at Court Herbert Colliery, near Neath, 1913. (*Western Mail and Echo Archives*)

Miners at Merthyr Vale Colliery. (*Western Mail and Echo Archives*)

Pit officials at Merthyr Vale. (*Western Mail and Echo Archives*)

William Philby (left) was only thirteen years old when this photograph was taken on the day he started work at Big Pit, Blaenavon, in 1903. He died of pneumonia in 1974. (*Western Mail and Echo Archives*)

A reminder of the days when coal merchants fetched their own supplies from Blaengarw Colliery, Aberdare. (*Western Mail and Echo Archives*)

Merchants collecting coal from Deep Navigation Ocean Colliery, Treharris, in 1905. (*Western Mail and Echo Archives*)

439 Lives Lost

Rescue workers with a canary waiting to go underground at
Universal Pit, Senghenydd, after Britain's worst pit disaster, which
claimed the lives of 439 men and boys in a vicious explosion on
16 October 1913. (All the illustrations in this section are from
contemporary postcards.)

A scene at Universal Colliery, Senghenydd, on the day of the disaster.

Some of the miners who volunteered to take part in the rescue operation.

The scene at the pithead.

Waiting for news of the victims at Senghenydd.

The coffin of one of the hundreds of victims of the disaster.

A Salvation Army officer comforts women waiting desperately for news of their loved ones.

Hardly a house in the village was not affected by the Senghenydd Pit disaster.

The funerals get underway.

Horse-drawn hearses passing through the crowded streets.

Salvation Army officers leading a funeral procession.

Hard Times

The 1920s and 1930s were tough, with strikes and lay-offs affecting the whole of the South Wales Coalfield. The hardship is reflected in the face of this miner, collecting either his pay or a redundancy notice at a South Wales pit.
(*Western Mail and Echo Archives*)

During the 1921 strike miners opened up levels in hillsides to outcrop bituminous coal seams to provide fuel for their homes. This outcrop was at Llwynypia level. (*Western Mail and Echo Archives*)

Miners at Gilfach Goch didn't even have time to change their clothes before going to the funeral of one of their mates, killed in a pit accident. (*Western Mail and Echo Archives*)

With newspapers not publishing because of the General Strike there was a dearth of photographs. This one, taken at the Modesty Mine, Ebbw Vale, shows the Jones and Ashman brothers who broke into the outcrop to get supplies for their families and fellow strikers. At Six Bells, Abertillery, two men were killed doing similar work around that time. The photograph was provided by the Department of Industry, National Museum of Wales, Nantgarw, and is published with the permission of Keith Jones, compiler of history books on Ebbw Vale.

On 25 October 1929 most of the South Wales Coalfield was on strike over a bid for a seven-hour week. Three miners who continued to work at Blaengarw needed a police escort of 170 officers to see them from the pit to home. One of the 'blacklegs' was apparently Will Whithead. Was he the man who later became president of the South Wales miners? (*Western Mail and Echo Archives*)

The Prince of Wales (second left) on a visit to the South Wales Coalfield in the 1920s. (*Western Mail and Echo Archives*)

A typical scene in a miner's cottage in South Wales before pithead baths were built. (*Western Mail and Echo Archives*)

A miner washing in front of a coal fire in South Wales. (*Western Mail and Echo Archives*)

Miners and their dogs at the Red Ash level, Blaina, in the 1930s. (*Western Mail and Echo Archives*)

Workers at Deep Pit, Nantyglo. (*Western Mail and Echo Archives*)

Strikers at the Parc Colliery in 1935. (*Western Mail and Echo Archives*)

Dan Evans of Pentre led the miners back to the surface at the end of an eight-day stay-down strike at Parc Colliery in 1935. The protest was over the use of blacklegs in a previous dispute. (*Western Mail and Echo Archives*)

This banner was carried in the hunger march from South Wales to London in 1936. (*Western Mail and Echo Archives*)

South Wales Marchers' Organising Council.

SOUTH WALES MINERS'
MARCH to LONDON

CALL TO ACTION! VOLUNTEERS WANTED!

Arising out of the pronouncement by A. J. COOK, 18/9/27, a Miners' March to London from S. Wales is being organised. The March will commence on the day Parliament opens—Nov. 8th, and the Marchers will arrive in London on Nov. 20th, where they will be received by an All London Working Class Demonstration.

The object of the March shall be two-fold, to arouse a Nationwide feeling concerning the Appalling Conditions in the Minefields created by the policy of the Government and the Coalowners, and to seek an interview with the Prime Minister, the Minister of Mines, the Minister of Labour, and the Minister of Health.

The purpose of such interview shall be :

1. To draw attention to the Chronic Destitution affecting Unemployed and Employed Miners arising out of the Failure of Private Enterprise in the Mining Industry.
2. To draw the attention of the Government to the persistent Closing of Mines, thus causing further widespread Unemployment.
3. To point out the consequences of the 8-hour Day.
4. To urge the Government to make Satisfactory Provision for the Employment of those Unemployed.
5. To demand State Aid to permit Guardians to more effectively Relieve Distress.
6. To protest against the Continuous Disqualification of Men and Women from Benefit at the Labour Exchange, and to urge More Adequate Scales of Benefit.
7. To press for a system of Adequate Pensioning of Miners over Sixty Years of age as a means of Reducing the Number of Unemployed.

Those wishing to Enrol as Recruits for this Historic March should make application at once to :

TRAGEDY OF THE MINEFIELDS MUST BE MADE KNOWN !

The call to action. (*Western Mail and Echo Archives*)

The hunger marchers passing through Runnymede, where King John signed the Magna Carta in 1215. (*Western Mail and Echo Archives*)

GARW OCEAN LODGE, S.W.M.F

You are heartily invited to attend

A RE-UNION DINNER
OF STAY-IN STRIKERS

at the

Workmen's Hall, Blaengarw, on
Thursday, October 24th. 1935,

at 6.30 p.m.

ALF DAVIES, Secretary.
R. PIERCE, Chairman.

An invitation to a reunion. (*Western Mail and Echo Archives*)

A group of miners at an unidentified coalface in South Wales. (*Western Mail and Echo Archives*)

Garw Colliery in the 1930s, set against a typical mining village with rows of terraced houses on the hillside. (*Western Mail and Echo Archives*)

Nationalisation Day

The day of the changeover, 1 January 1947.
(*Western Mail and Echo*)

Duffryn Rhondda Colliery on the day the pits were nationalised, 1 January 1947. (*Western Mail and Echo*)

A section of the crowd at Duffryn Rhondda on Nationalisation Day. (*Western Mail and Echo*)

The first National Coal Board, the new bosses of Britain's 680,000 miners. Left to right: Sir Charles Ellis, T.E.B. Young, Sir Charles Reid, Sir Arthur Street, Lord Hyndley (chairman), Lord Citrins, Mr Jelfers, Mr Ebby and L.H.R. Lowe. (*National Coal Board*)

Miners singing the Welsh national anthem on the eve of Nationalisation Day. (*Western Mail and Echo*)

Vesting boards like this went up at collieries throughout Britain on 1 January 1947. This one was at Naval Colliery, Penygraig. (*Western Mail and Echo*)

Towards the end of the Second World War some men were conscripted as miners; they were known as Bevin Boys, after Ernest Bevin, the Labour minister in Churchill's coalition government. This group of Bevin Boys were working at Oakwood Colliery, Blackwood, around 1944. (*Bevin Boys Association, Warwick Taylor, 01308 861488*)

Customers queuing for coal at a Cardiff siding during the great blizzard of March 1947. The compiler of this book, John O'Sullivan, who was twelve years old at the time, remembers dragging home bags of coal on a home-made sledge from the Cadoxton sidings at Barry for his family and neighbours in nearby Harvey Street. (*Western Mail and Echo*)

Miners from all over South Wales lobbied Parliament in January 1959, in protest against the closure of seven pits in the South Western Division. (*Western Mail and Echo*)

Protesters in London in January 1959. (*Western Mail and Echo*)

Women joined the fight for jobs in 1959. These placard holders were Mrs Cyril Parry (left), wife of the chairman of the Morlais National Union of Mineworkers' Lodge, and May Llewellyn, an executive member of the British Peace Committee. (*Western Mail and Echo*)

Some of the people who joined the celebrations when the coke ovens were commissioned at Nantgarw in the 1950s. (*Western Mail and Echo*)

Maritime Colliery, Pontypridd, was sunk by John Edmunds in 1841 and finally closed in 1961. It was the first pit in the South Wales Coalfield to have by-product coke ovens. (*Department of Industry, National Museum of Wales, Nantgarw*)

Glamorgan Colliery, Llwynypia. (*Western Mail Archives*)

The South Wales Area NUM with their banner, which was unveiled in 1955. (*Western Mail and Echo*)

Decade of Sorrow

Grim-faced rescue workers at Six Bells Colliery, Abertillery, on 28 June 1960, the day
that forty-five men died in an underground explosion. (*Western Mail and Echo*)

Six Bells Colliery, Abertillery. (*Western Mail and Echo*)

Another view of Six Bells Colliery. (*Western Mail and Echo*)

Rescue workers take time out for a cigarette and a rest before returning underground after the explosion at Six Bells Colliery, Abertillery, on 28 June 1960. (*Western Mail and Echo*)

Officials prepare to go underground the day after the disaster. (*Western Mail and Echo*)

Rescue workers grabbed any chance to find something to eat. (*Western Mail and Echo*)

The anxious wait went on well into the night. (*Western Mail and Echo*)

A mother nurses her baby Welsh shawl fashion as she waits at the pithead with other wives and children for news of the disaster. (*Western Mail and Echo*)

The anxiously waiting loved ones feared the worst. (*Western Mail and Echo*)

Silently waiting for news. (*Western Mail and Echo*)

The anxiety can be seen on the faces of the women and children. (*Western Mail and Echo*)

An anxious group of relatives and friends wait for news of the rescue efforts. (*Western Mail and Echo*)

Crowds gather round as a policeman briefs reporters, including the dark-haired Jack Parker of the South Wales Echo. In 1969 Parker was in charge of the government press team at the Investiture of the Prince of Wales at Caernarvon Castle. (*Western Mail and Echo*)

Lord Brecon, Minister of State for Welsh Affairs, talks to rescue workers. (*Western Mail and Echo*)

Civic leaders joined the funeral procession. (*Western Mail and Echo*)

Some of the five thousand men who walked to the cemetery. (*Western Mail and Echo*)

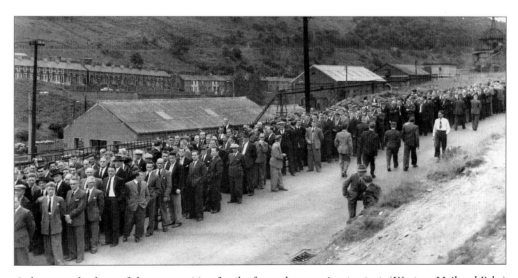

Sadness on the faces of the men waiting for the funeral procession to start. (*Western Mail and Echo*)

SOUTH WALES E

FOUNDED 1884   **SATURDAY JULY 2 1960**

They march through the valley of

● Some of the five thousand miners moving silently down the road to pay their last respects to their dead co

A NATION'S MILE
SORROW

Another £1,700 for Fund

WITH only the sound of their echoing footsteps breaking the sorrowful silence, thousands of miners marched at Six Bells today in a vast demonstration of the brotherhood of the men of the pit.

From all parts of the South Wales coalfield they came to lead the funeral procession of 26 of the men killed in the Arrael Griffin Colliery disaster.

For a mile they stretched down the roadway, cut 'ike a ledge in the mountainside from the New Cemetery, Brynithel, to Six Bells.

Above the ill-fated pit with

**By JACK PARKER
and
TERRY CAMPBELL**

The Rev. Llywelyn Williams, M.P., Mr. Ness Edwards M.P.,

ing the sharp incline along which so many tragic journeys have been held this week. Up to the main road of Six Bells where people stood silent and watching on their doorsteps.

No banners

and bands

Without banners or bands the vast contingent followed behind. A solid phalanx of silent sor-

LATE CITY

3d.

Home means more with FURNITURE from THE ROATH FURNISHING CO CITY RD. CARDIFF Tel 30421

ence

of Six Bells.

Mr. Bevan critically ill say doctors

MR. Aneurin Bevan is critically ill, his doctors said today. The 62-year-old deputy leader of the Opposition had a "very unsatisfactory night."

A Labour Party spokesman said today:

"In the circumstances, Miss Jennie Lee has decided to cancel her speaking engagement at Cannock (Staffs.) and to remain at Asheridge with Mr. Bevan."

Mr. Bevan lives at Asheridge Farm, near Chesham, Bucks. The most recent bulletin on his health stated that he was recovering from a blood clot in the leg.

Last December he had a major abdominal operation at the Royal Free Hospital, London.

Mr. A. J. Lush, of Tredegar, an inspector of schools in Monmouthshire, who has been with Mr. Bevan every week-end during his convalescence, is with him again this week-end.

His agent

He left Tredegar last night. He was for many years Mr. Bevan's agent in Ebbw Vale.

In April Mr. Bevan's recuperative holiday was postponed because of a slight setback in health. It was described as "one of the upsets that can be expected following a major operation of the kind Mr. Bevan has had." He was again in bed for several days.

Mr. Lush, one of his closest friends, disclosed that one of the doctors had said that he had "never seen such a magnificent fighter" as Mr. Bevan.

"It was Nye's fighting spirit that pulled him through," said Mr. Lush.

In May Mr. Bevan had his holiday in the sun, but to avoid publicity the destination was not disclosed.

MR. BEVAN

Explosion danger on blazing ship

Singapore, Saturday. — The crew of the 9,884-ton British vessel Bennchaie temporarily abandoned ship in Singapore outer harbour today in the face of fire and a possible explosion. They went back on board later.

According to harbour board sources there were 69 boxes of highly dangerous electrical detonators in the hold. Flooding of the engine room prevented the fire from spreading. — Reuter.

MISSING GIRL FOUND

Kathleen Rathbone, the 12-year-old girl who had been missing from her home in Edward Road, Christchurch, since Thursday, was found at Lymington (Hants) today with a 21-year-old youth. A policeman saw them walking along a road.

LATE NEWS

Telephone 33022

Strike will stop Eire steamers

UNLESS strike notices served by Dublin shipping clerks and due to expire on Monday are withdrawn, steamer services across the Irish Sea will be affected.

The British and Irish Steam Packet Co. issued a statement in Liverpool today saying that as a result of the dispute it

The front page of the *South Wales Echo* on 2 July 1960, the day of the funeral of the Six Bells disaster victims. Sharing the headlines was Nye Bevan, MP for Ebbw Vale and founder of the National Health Service. He died a few days later. (*National Newspaper Library*)

Mourners wind their way through the narrow streets. (*Western Mail and Echo*)

Bowed heads at the graveside. (*Western Mail and Echo*)

Killer Explosion

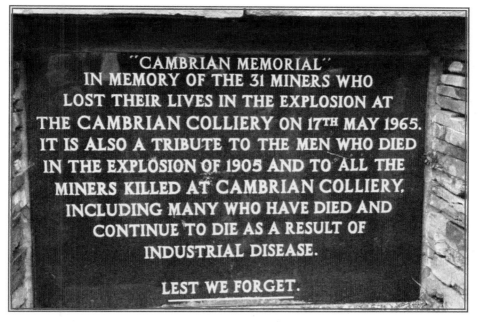

This plaque was unveiled on the thirtieth anniversary of the Cambrian Colliery disaster. A memorial garden now stands on the site of the pit where thirty-one men died on 17 May 1965. In a previous explosion at the colliery, on 10 March 1905, the death toll was also thirty-one. (*Western Mail and Echo*)

Some of the men who volunteered to take part in the rescue operation. (*Western Mail and Echo*)

Ambulances lined up on the road leading to the colliery, waiting to take away the dead and injured. (*Western Mail and Echo*)

Women comforted each other as they waited for news. (*Western Mail and Echo*)

Anxious women and children waiting for news of their loved ones. (*Western Mail and Echo*)

The pain of the waiting is etched on the faces of the women at the pithead. (*Western Mail and Echo*)

Schoolchildren watch as more rescue volunteers arrive at Cambrian Colliery. (*Western Mail and Echo*)

Anxious villagers wait for news from the pit. (*Western Mail and Echo*)

Lord Robins (right), chairman of the National Coal Board, with area general manager G. Blackmore (centre) and H. Collins, production director of NCB. (*Western Mail and Echo*)

Several dignitaries visited the scene of the disaster. They included (left to right) A.H. Kellett, chairman of the South Western District of the National Coal Board; John Morris, MP for Aberavon, who worked in the Ministry of Power; Jim Griffiths, MP for Llanelli and Secretary of State for Wales, and Dan Murphy, Mayor-elect of the Rhondda. (*Western Mail and Echo*)

Jim Griffiths, Secretary of State for Wales, talked to miners outside the Assembly Hall, Clydach Vale, which was used as a mortuary for the thirty-one bodies. (*Western Mail and Echo*)

Will Whitehead, president of the South Wales miners, thanking Salvation Army officers for the support they offered to the families after the disaster. (*Western Mail and Echo*)

A man and child listen to news of the disaster on a transistor radio. (*Western Mail and Echo*)

NAME	ADDRESS	AGE
A. Colcombe.	87, Marian St. Clydach. V.	44
D. Evans.	4, Bryntawel. Bl'nclydach	28
W.I. Thomas.	13, Francis St. Clydach Vale	
L. May.	347, Brithwenydd Trealaw	33
A. Newman.	3, Bryn Terr. Blaenclydach	46
I. Jacobs.	83, Ynyscynon Rd. Trealaw	45
J. Channing.	31, Brook St. Williamstown	46
E.L Rees.	57, Edmundstown Rd. Penrhiwfer	48
V Nicholas.	53, Maddock St. Bl'nclydach	51
R. Daniels.	108, Park St. Clydach Vale	34
G. Thomas	31, Jones St. Blaenclydach	28
I. Morgan	Flat 2 New Century Rd. Trealaw	32
D. Price	4 Llwynypia Rd. Tonypandy	42
T. Williams	78 High St. Clydach Vale	27
R.J. Roberts	25 Court St. Tonypandy	55
S. Williams	74 Ely St. "	
K. Davies	8 Railway Terr Blaenclydach	26
E. Williams	17. Rowling St. Williamstown	51
E.W Burnett	30 Caeglass Penrhiwfer	46
T.J. Harris	4 Sunny Bank Blaenclydach	
R. Hucker	103 Park St. Clydach Vale	
R Flower	83 Marian St. "	45
D. Calvert	96 Charles St. Tonypandy	40
D. Griffith	"	43
R. Gregson	154 Dunraven St. Treherbert	21
H. Lee	70 High St. Clydach Vale	56
R. Arnold	26 Pontypridd. Rd. Porth	48
H. Pope	106 Wern St. Clydach Vale	50
G. Davies	170 Court St. Tonypandy	24
E. Breeze	[Manager]	
L. Williams	[Undermanager]	

The Roll of Honour. (*Western Mail and Echo*)

The funeral procession passes the Pandy Hotel, an area closely linked to the industry's history as it was the scene of several battles between police and miners during the 1911 strike. (*Western Mail and Echo*)

The tears flowed freely as the funeral cortège passed the grieving crowds on the way to Trealaw Cemetery. (*Western Mail and Echo*)

The scene at the graveside at Trealaw Cemetery. (*Western Mail and Echo*)

The Revd Ceredig Thomas prepares for the graveside service at Salem Welsh Baptist Chapel, Ton-Teg, for Cambrian manager Ernest Breeze, who died in the disaster, along with thirty of his men. The pit closed twenty months later. (*Western Mail and Echo*)

Suffer Little Children

The prayer that comforted grieving villagers after 144 people,
including 116 children, died when a colliery waste tip slipped,
crushing a school and houses in the village of Aberfan at
9.16 a.m. on Friday 21 October 1966. (*Western Mail and Echo*)

Men searching for victims and survivors in the ruins of the school. (*Western Mail and Echo*)

The search continued well into the night. (*Western Mail and Echo*)

As dawn broke on 22 October 1966, the full horror of the disaster became known. (*Western Mail and Echo*)

Labour Prime Minister Harold Wilson leaving the school where the children died. (*Western Mail and Echo*)

The Queen walks through the grieving village. On her right is Councillor Jim Williams, who lost five relatives in the disaster. (*Royal Rota photograph*)

The Queen talks to the village bobby, Police Constable Vic Jones, and Detective Superintendent John Parkman, head of the Regional Crime Squad. The Mayor of Merthyr, Stan Davies, who launched the Aberfan Disaster Fund, is also in the group. (*Royal Rota photograph*)

Support for the Aberfan families came from many quarters, including the Sisters Bonaventure and Irene, of St Joseph of Annecy, Llantarnam Abbey, Gwent. (*Western Mail and Echo*)

Merthyr Vale Colliery, which produced the waste that had formed the disaster tip on the nearby hillside above Aberfan. (*Western Mail and Echo*)

Merthyr councillors were among the thousands who walked to the Aberfan Cemetery on the day that eighty-one of the victims, all but one of them children, were buried. The compiler of this book, John O'Sullivan, covered the disaster for the Daily Mail and is seen leaning against the wall on the right. (*Western Mail and Echo*)

The memorial at Aberfan Cemetery, where most of the young victims of the disaster are buried in a mass grave. (*Western Mail and Echo*)

The memorial overlooks the village. (*Western Mail and Echo*)

Miners at Brynlliw Colliery, Gorseinon, waiting anxiously for news of 'Butties' trapped by a roof fall in the 1960s. (*Western Mail and Echo*)

There was a lively NUM meeting at Porthcawl in 1969 when the question of shorter hours was on the agenda. (*Western Mail and Echo*)

Striking miners lobbied the NUM delegates meeting at The Pavilion, Porthcawl, in 1969. (*Western Mail and Echo*)

The scene inside The Pavilion. (*Western Mail and Echo*)

Miners from Townhill Colliery, Rhondda, and Lady Windsor Colliery, Ynysybwll, picketed the Tymawr Colliery, Hopkinstown, where production continued during the 1969 strike. (*Western Mail and Echo*)

Miners who stayed at the surface while thirty-five of their mates staged a sit-in strike at International Colliery, Blaengarw, in the early 1960s. (*Western Mail and Echo*)

Men walked out on strike at Trelewis Drift Mine, Treharris, after a manager was alleged to have used a four-letter word against an NUM lodge official. (*Western Mail and Echo*)

They had lost their jobs, but were still smiling. Miners decided to hold a party after the Navigation Colliery, Wattstown, closed down in December 1968. (*Western Mail and Echo*)

The Government Falls

The badge of the South Wales Area NUM. (*Western Mail and Echo Archives*)

Miners from Glynnen Colliery, near Newbridge, kept warm while picketing Rogerstone power station during the miners' strike in 1972. The strike helped to bring down the Conservative government led by Ted Heath. (*Western Mail and Echo*)

Pickets at Penrhiwceiber in 1972. (*Western Mail and Echo*)

The mass pickets at places like Penrhiwceiber led to the Conservative government in the 1980s introducing legislation restricting the number of pickets allowed at any one time. These men were trying to stop a van containing safety workers. (*Western Mail and Echo*)

Miners in the lamp room at Merthyr Vale Colliery around the time of the 1972 strike, which led to Ted Heath's government rationing power and putting industry on a three-day week. (*Western Mail and Echo*)

Pickets tried to persuade workers at the NCB's headquarters in Llanishen, Cardiff, to join the 1972 strike. (*Western Mail and Echo*)

Pickets surround a car at the NUM headquarters at Llanishen, Cardiff. (*Western Mail and Echo*)

There was a mass rally by strikers in Cardiff in January 1972. (*Western Mail and Echo*)

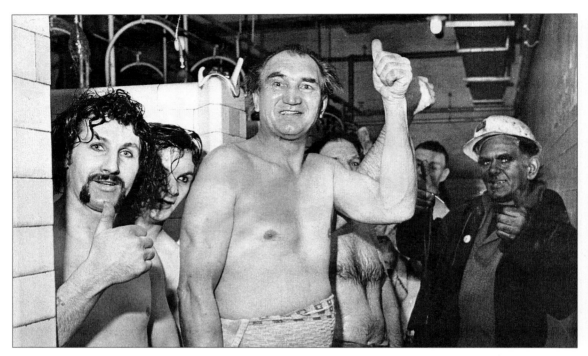

Miners at Bedwas Colliery, on the eve of another strike in February 1974. (*Western Mail and Echo*)

In the early 1970s widows of miners lobbied miners at Windsor Colliery, Abertrider, asking for some of the miners' free coal allowance to be handed over to them. (*Western Mail and Echo*)

There were happy smiles at Penallta Colliery, Bargoed, in June 1979 when the pit was taken off the jeopardy list. The news was broken by NCB area director Lister Walker (left) and Glyn Williams, president of the South Wales miners. (*Western Mail and Echo*)

Thumbs up from the men of Treforgan Colliery, Trynant, in the late 1970s. They had just been told that their pit had been taken off the closure list. (*Western Mail and Echo*)

Miners from Oglive Colliery took their fight against closure in the mid-1970s to the House of Commons. (*Western Mail and Echo*)

Some of the delegates at an annual conference of the South Wales NUM at Porthcawl in the troubled 1970s. (*Western Mail and Echo*)

The 50mph Man Ride train was introduced to the Abertillery New Mine in the late 1970s and it cut travelling time to the coalface by 50 minutes. (*NCB photograph*)

A radio-controlled coal shearing machine was introduced at Markham Colliery, Blackwood, in the 1970s. (*Western Mail and Echo*)

Max Boyce, who worked at a colliery before he became a world-famous folk singer, is seen here above the Rhondda Valley. His lyrics 'In our little valley, they've closed the colliery down and the pithead bath's a supermarket now' provide a fitting epitaph for the industry in Wales. (*Western Mail and Echo*)

Pit ponies were brought to the surface at Penrhiwceiber during the mining strikes in the 1970s. (*Western Mail and Echo*)

The Year-Long Strike

The end of an era for the Rhondda Valley. (*Western Mail and Echo*)

The end of a sit-in strike at Nantgarw Colliery in 1983. (*Western Mail and Echo*)

Miners' national president Arthur Scargill leading a march through Cardiff in March 1984, after miners throughout Britain started a twelve-month strike against threatened pit closures. (*Western Mail and Echo*)

Arthur Scargill addressing a mass rally at Sophia Gardens, Cardiff. (*Western Mail and Echo*)

On another visit to South Wales, Arthur Scargill walked through Ystrad Rhondda. (*Western Mail and Echo*)

Wives of miners voiced their anger at Prime Minister Margaret Thatcher when she attended the Wales Conservative Party Conference at The Pavilion, Porthcawl, in 1984. (*Western Mail and Echo*)

Nurses showed their solidarity with the miners during the 1984 strike. (*Western Mail and Echo*)

A miner makes a point while picketing at Penrhiwceiber Colliery. (*Western Mail and Echo*)

Police and pickets clashed at Marine Colliery, Cwm, Ebbw Vale. (*Western Mail and Echo*)

Members of the Maerdy Lodge at a mass rally. (*Western Mail and Echo*)

The Mardy Colliery Band kept playing during the strike. (*Western Mail and Echo*)

After the strike, history was made when Mardy Colliery and Tower Colliery were linked underground. It marked the end of coal being brought to the surface in the Rhondda Valley. (*Western Mail and Echo*)

While a black cloud hung over the future of the South Wales Coalfield, miners at Trelewis Drift Mine continued to break records. (*Western Mail and Echo*)

Big Pit at Blaenavon is now a museum where visitors can experience what happened underground and on the surface. The pit was opened as a tourist attraction by actor Windsor Davies. (*Western Mail and Echo*)

Among the first groups to visit Big Pit were children of Class Five from Ysgol Gymraeg, Pentrebane, Cardiff. (*Western Mail and Echo*)

The End of an Era

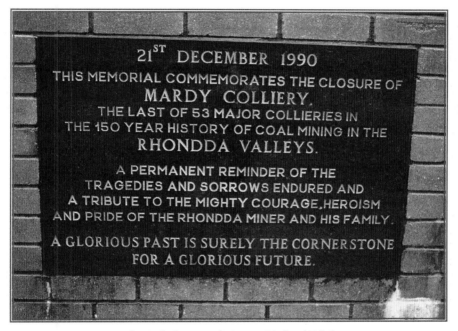

The end of an era. (*Western Mail and Echo*)

A march was organised to mark the closure of Mardy Colliery. (*Western Mail and Echo*)

Some of the six hundred miners who lost their jobs when the Blaenant Colliery in West Glamorgan closed in 1991. (*Western Mail and Echo*)

Children who were not even born when the last coal was cut in their valley marched in January 1996 from Pantgog to Blaengarw to mark the tenth anniversary of the closure of the Garw Colliery. (*Western Mail and Echo*)

Residents in Caerphilly fought plans for opencast mining on the mountain overlooking the town. (*Western Mail and Echo*)

Champagne corks popped when the Welsh Office rejected plans by the Clay Colliery Company to extract 200,000 tonnes of coal from Wernddu claypits on Caerphilly Mountain. (*Western Mail and Echo*)

The Freedom of the City

Ex-miners carrying their banner from Cardiff Castle with pride. (*Western Mail and Echo*)

Rickie Ormonde was affectionately known as the People's Lord Mayor and one of the proudest moments of his life came when he conferred the Freedom of Cardiff on the South Wales miners on 1 April 1995. Holding the scroll of honour is NUM president George Rees. (*Western Mail and Echo*)

Families from the mining valleys gathered at Cardiff Castle before marching to the City Hall for the Freedom Ceremony. (*Western Mail and Echo*)

Part of the crowd at the Freedom Ceremony in the City Hall. (*Western Mail and Echo*)

Pendyrus Male Choir sang with gusto at the Freedom Ceremony. (*Western Mail and Echo*)

It was the South Wales miners who made Cardiff the greatest coal-exporting port in the world and they richly deserved the Freedom of the Capital City of Wales. Their links go back more than a hundred years. This was the scene at the miners' road race in 1928. (*Western Mail and Echo*)

The winners are chaired at the end of the 1928 road race. (*Western Mail and Echo*)

A band leads the miners and their families through Queen Street, Cardiff, on a Gala Day in 1976. (*Western Mail and Echo*)

Jenny Lee MP, Nye Bevan's widow, addressing a miners' rally at Sophia Gardens in 1962. (*Western Mail and Echo*)

When the 14th Miners' Gala took place in Cardiff in 1967, the guest speaker was Ray Gunter MP (second from right). Others in the picture include Ted Rowlands MP (second left) and Dai Francis (left), the highly respected General Secretary of the South Wales Area NUM. He calmed down many disputes with his motto: 'Keep your powder dry'. (*Western Mail and Echo*)

In 1949 South Wales had 254 pits and 113,000 miners. Today we have 1 pit and 370 miners

Black Wednesday

THE LAST PIT IN WALES: *Tower Hirwaun Colliery near Aberdare will soon be our sole remaining mine*

The destruction of an industry. (*Western Mail and Echo*)

Glofa Twr
The last deep mine in Wales
Tower Colliery

The victory won by the miners of Tower Colliery, led by Tyrone O'Sullivan. (*Western Mail and Echo*)

Walking to victory: Tyrone O'Sullivan, his wife Elaine and Ann Clwyd, MP for Cynon Valley. (*Western Mail and Echo*)

Kim Howells, MP for Pontypridd (centre), and Ted Rowlands, MP for Merthyr (right), joined the fight to save Tower from closure. (*Western Mail and Echo*)

Miners at Tower Colliery dipping a cloth in a red liquid to re-enact the flying of the Red Flag ceremony at Hirwaun in 1831. Tyrone O'Sullivan is in the centre. (*Western Mail and Echo*)

Miners' President Arthur Scargill was among those who walked for Tower. (*Western Mail and Echo*)

In 1992 the miners at Tower were hailed as Britain's new tunnelling champions – one of the reasons why they deserved to keep their pit open. (*Western Mail and Echo*)

The miners of Tower celebrated their victory with beer, not champagne. Crown Buckley breweries donated a thousand cans of beer for the occasion. (*Western Mail and Echo*)

Rest in Peace

The tomb of the Unknown Soldier is in Westminster Abbey,
London. The graves of the Unknown Miners, victims of the
underground explosion which killed 290 men and boys at
Albion Colliery in 1894, are found at Llanfabon Cemetery.
(*Western Mail and Echo*)

Lest We Forget

The first recorded major disaster included in the South Wales Directory was at Cwmllynfell Colliery in 1825, when 59 men died. The exact date is not given. Following is a list of other major disasters which are recorded in the directory. Hundreds of other miners also died in individual accidents in the pits.

1837
18 June Blaina Colliery 21

1838
28 Nov. Cinder Pit 16

1844
1 Jan. Dinas Middle Pit 12
2 Aug. Cwmbach 28

1846
14 Jan. Risca Black Vein 35
11 June Victoria E. Vale 11

1849
11 Aug. Lletty Shenkin 52

1850
14 Dec. New Duffryn Pit 13

1852
10 May Middle Duffryn Pit 65
10 May Gwendraeth 26

1853
12 Mar. Risca Black Vein 10

1856
20 May Cwmavon 12
3 July Old Coal Pit 11
15 July Cymmer Old Pit 114

1857
27 May Tyr Nicholas 13

1858
25 Feb. Lower Duffryn Pit 19
28 May Bryndu 12
14 Oct. Primrose, Swansea Valley 14

1859
5 April Neath Chain Pit 26

1860
6 Nov. Lower Duffryn 12
1 Dec. Risca Black Vein 142

1861
8 Mar. Blaengarw 13

1862
19 Feb. Gethin 47

1863
17 Oct. Morfa 39
24 Dec. Gin Pit 14

1865
16 June Bedwellty pits 26
20 Dec. Upper Gethin Pit 34

1868
8 Nov. Ferndale 178

1869
10 June Ferndale 53

1870
14 Feb. Morfa 30
23 July Charles Pit 19

1871
14 Feb. Pentre 38

1872
10 Jan. Oakwood 11
2 Mar. Victoria 19
8 Mar. Wernfach 18

1875
4 Dec. New Tredegar 23
6 Dec. Llan Pit 16

1876
18 Dec. Cwmtillery 23

1877
8 Mar. Worcester Pit 18

1878
11 Sept. Prince of Wales, Abercarn 268

1879
13 Jan. Dinas Middle Pit 64
22 Sept. Waunlwyd 84

1880
15 July Risca New Pit 120
10 Dec. Naval 101

1884
16 Jan. Cwmavon 10
27 Jan. Penygraig 14
8 Nov. Pochin 14

1885
23 Dec. Mardy, Rhondda 81

1887
18 Feb. Standard 39

1890
6 Feb. Llanerch 176
8 Mar. Morfa 87

1892
12 Aug. Great Western 58
26 Aug. Park Slip 112

1894
23 June Albion Colliery 290

1896
26 Jan. Tylorston 57

1899
18 Aug. Llest 19

1901
24 May Universal, Senghenydd 82
10 Sept. Llanbradach 12

1902
– Mclaren No. 1 16

1905
19 Mar. Cambrian Navigation 31
5 July National 119

1913
14 Oct. Universal, Senghenydd 439

1927
1 Mar. Marine 52

1932
25 Jan. Llwynipia 11

1941
10 July Rhigos No. 4 16

1960
28 June Six Bells, Abertillery 45

1962
– Tower Colliery 9

1965
17 May Cambrian Navigation 31

1966
21 Oct. Aberfan tip slide 144
(including 116 children)

1972
– Cynheidre 6

Acknowledgements

John O'Sullivan wishes to thank everyone who has helped him to compile this book. Special thanks are due to the following: the *Western Mail and Echo*, their generations of photographers and librarians; Bryn Jones and the staff at Cardiff Central Library Local Studies Department; Pontypridd Library; Treorchy Library; Abertillery Library; Keith Jones, compiler of history books on Ebbw Vale; the Department of Industry, National Museum of Wales, Nantgarw; the South Wales Mining Library, Swansea; Ray Lawrence, the South Wales Coalfield Directory; the Labour Museum, Manchester; Tyrone O'Sullivan of Tower Colliery; Barry Tobin; Carys Wheelan; and the late Ness Edwards MP.